A My Name Is Annabel

A Sesame Street Alphabet Book

By Michaela Muntean
Illustrated by Tom Brannon

Featuring Jim Henson's Sesame Street Muppets

A SESAME STREET/GOLDEN PRESS BOOK
Published by Western Publishing Company, Inc.
in conjunction with Children's Television Workshop

A My name is Annabel. This is my alligator.
When we go out, he always orders apples from the waiter.

B My name is Betty Lou. This is Barkley and Big Bird.
We each have something special that's our favorite B word!

C My name is Cookie Monster. Me like cakes. And cookies, too.
My very favorite C words are the ones that me can chew!

D My name is Duncan. I make doughnuts every day.
Jelly-filled or chocolate-dipped, one dime is all you pay.

E My name is Ernie. What do all those elephants eat
That gives them such enormous ears and such enormous feet?

F My name is Ferdinand. On each foot I have five toes;
On each hand I have five fingers, but I only have one nose.

G My name is Grover. While I was eating some green grapes,
This cute and naughty little goat ate my granny's drapes!

H My name is Herry. Hats make the best disguise.
I have hats in every color, every shape, and every size.

I My name is Isabel. I want to eat my ice cream cone,
But this insect just keeps bugging me, and won't leave me alone!

J My name is Jack. When I juggle jelly beans,
I like to wear my jacket and my favorite old blue jeans.

K My name is Katie. I know two kangaroos,
Who like to go, every day, shopping for new shoes.

L My name is Linda Lou. I am drinking lemonade. I like to sip it slowly while I'm sitting in the shade.

M My name is Mumford. With this most amazing mop,
I will clean up all the mud we've tracked into this shop.

N My name is Norbert. I can count to number nine.
I have counted nine fine monsters waiting in this line.

O My name is Oscar. I like gloppy cold oatmeal,
But only when it's mixed with yucchy orange peel.

P My name is Prairie Dawn. I like pickles, pears, and peas,
But my very favorite P words are, "Pass the pancakes, please!"

Q I am the queen of quilts, and the king thinks I am wise
To have quilts in every color, every shape, and every size!

R My name is Rosie. I love the rodeo.
I ride around the ring and do rope tricks in the show.

S My name is Snuffle-Upagus. My friends just call me Snuffie. If I don't wear my socks and scarf, my snuffle gets all stuffy.

T We are two Twiddlebugs riding on a train.
We have two round-trip tickets to Tizzleberry, Maine.

U I'm Ukelele Luke. **V** I'm Violin Vance.
W I'm Washboard Will. Pick your partners and let's dance.

X My name is Xavier. I can play the xylophone.
I like the tunes I play, but they make my family groan!

Y My name is Yolanda. I have yards of yellow yarn.
I have enough to knit a sweater for a barn!

Z My name is Zelda May. I am visiting the zoo.
When you meet my friend the zebra, then our alphabet is through!

ABCDEFGHIJ